T0069308

Vol. 2149

BEETHOVEN
SELECTED PIANO PIECES

FOR EARLY INTERMEDIATE
TO INTERMEDIATE LEVEL

35 Selections from
Bagatelles, German Dances,
Minuets, Sonatas, Sonatinas and more

ISBN 978-1-5400-8984-7

G. SCHIRMER, Inc.

DISTRIBUTED BY

7777 W. BLUEMOUND RD. P.O. BOX 13819 MILWAUKEE, WI 53213

For all works contained herein:
Unauthorized copying, arranging, adapting, recording, Internet posting, public performance,
or other distribution of the music in this publication is an infringement of copyright.
Infringers are liable under the law.

Visit Hal Leonard Online at
www.halleonard.com

Contact us:
Hal Leonard
7777 West Bluemound Road
Milwaukee, WI 53213
Email: info@halleonard.com

In Europe, contact:
Hal Leonard Europe Limited
42 Wigmore Street
Marylebone, London, W1U 2RN
Email: info@halleonardeurope.com

In Australia, contact:
Hal Leonard Australia Pty. Ltd.
4 Lentara Court
Cheltenham, Victoria, 3192 Australia
Email: info@halleonard.com.au

CONTENTS

ALLEGRETTO
in B minor

Ludwig van Beethoven
WoO 61

sempre legato

BAGATELLE
in E-flat Major

Ludwig van Beethoven
Op. 33, No. 1

Andante grazioso, quasi Allegretto (♩.=56)

BAGATELLE
in F Major

Ludwig van Beethoven
Op. 33, No. 3

Allegretto ($\downarrow\cdot = 84$)

BAGATELLE
in G minor

Ludwig van Beethoven
Op. 119, No. 1

Allegretto

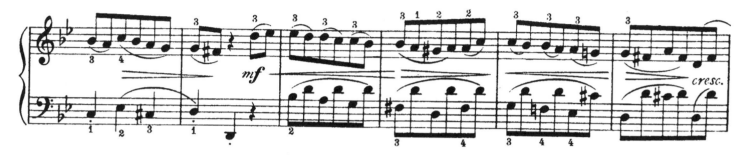

BAGATELLE
in C Major

Ludwig van Beethoven
Op. 119, No. 8

Moderato cantabile

BAGATELLE
in A minor

Ludwig van Beethoven
Op. 119, No. 9

Vivace moderato

BAGATELLE
in C Major

Ludwig van Beethoven
Op. 126, No. 5

ÉCOSSAISE
in G Major

Ludwig van Beethoven
WoO 23

Allegretto

ÉCOSSAISE
in E-flat Major

Ludwig van Beethoven
WoO 86

WALTZ
in D Major

Ludwig van Beethoven
WoO 85

GERMAN DANCE
in E-flat Major

Ludwig van Beethoven
WoO 8, No. 5

Fine

Trio

D. C.

GERMAN DANCE
in G Major

Ludwig van Beethoven
WoO 8, No. 6

Trio

GERMAN DANCE
in C Major

Ludwig van Beethoven
WoO 8, No. 7

Fine

Trio

D. C.

GERMAN DANCE
in D Major

Ludwig van Beethoven
WoO 13, No. 1

Fine

Trio

D. C.

GERMAN DANCE
in B-flat Major

Ludwig van Beethoven
WoO 13, No. 2

Fine

Trio

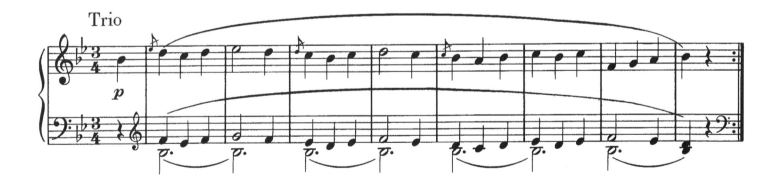

D.C.

GERMAN DANCE
in B-flat Major

Ludwig van Beethoven
WoO 13, No. 6

Fine

Trio

D.C.

GERMAN DANCE
in E-flat Major

Ludwig van Beethoven
WoO 13, No. 9

Fine

Trio

D.C.

SEVEN LÄNDLER

Ludwig van Beethoven
WoO 11

1

2

3

4

5

6

7

CODA

MINUET
in G Major

Ludwig van Beethoven
WoO 10, No. 2

Fine

Trio

D. C.

MINUET
in E-flat Major

Ludwig van Beethoven
WoO 82

Minuetto da capo

RONDO
in C Major

Ludwig van Beethoven
Op. 51, No. 1

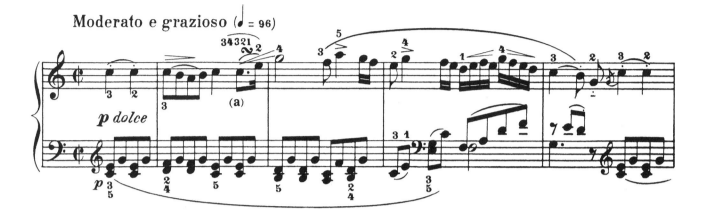

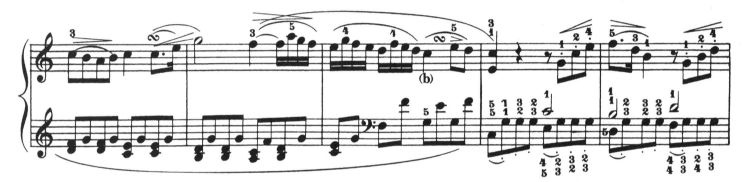

a)

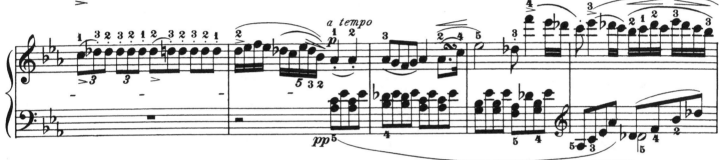

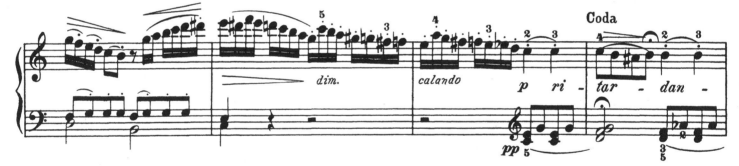

RONDO
in C Major

Ludwig van Beethoven
WoO 48

Allegretto

*May also be played:

SONATA

in G minor

Edited and fingered by
Sigmund Lebert and Hans von Bülow

Ludwig van Beethoven
Op. 49, No. 1

Abbreviations: M. T., signifies Main Theme; S. T., Sub Theme; Cl. T., Closing Theme; D. G., Development-group;
R., Return; Tr., Transition; Md. T., Mid-Theme; Ep., Episode; App., Appendix.

a) *mfp* signifies: the first note *mf*, the following ones *p*.

b) With the comma we indicate places where the player must perceptibly mark the end of a rhythmic group or section, by lifting the last note just before its time-value expires, although the composer wrote no rest.

c)

d) The left hand more subdued than the right, but still accenting the first of each pair of 16th- notes (i. e.: the bass notes proper) somewhat more than the second.

e)

f) Here and in the next measure the left hand should accent only the first note in each group of 16th-notes somewhat more than the others, but in all cases less than the soprano.

g) As at d.)

h) In these three measures as at f.)

a) As at (f) on the preceding Page.

b)

c) The left hand here again more subdued than the right.

d) As at (a).

e) In these twelve measures the first and third notes in each group of 16th notes should be made somewhat more prominent than the other notes, yet always in subordination to the melody, excepting the tones marked >

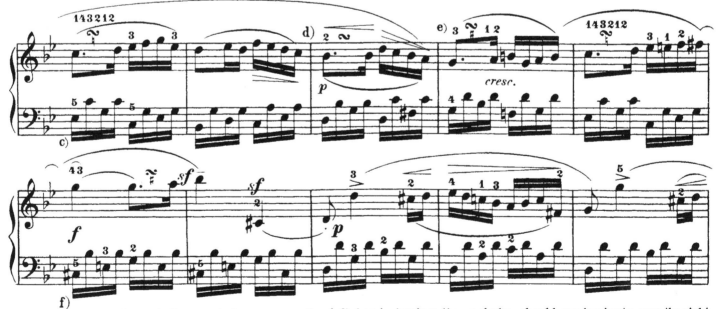

a) From here through the next 6 measures the left hand, having the melody, should predominate over the right, and, where it has 2 tones, chiefly accentuate the higher one.

b) As on first Page.

c) The next 5 measures as on first Page.

d) Doubtless literally meant neither for ♪♪♪♪ nor for: ♪♪♪♪ but ♪♪♪♪

e) This and the following turns again as on first Page.

f) From here onward as on second Page.

Rondo.
Allegro. (♩. = 92.)

a)

b) Proceed only after a rest.

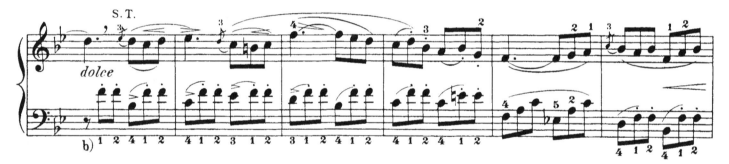

a) In these groups of 16th-notes, accent each first note slightly more than the 5 following, while subordinating all to the soprano. These same accented notes, too, (except in the fourth measure) should be held down during the second 16th-note.

b) Also subordinate this accompaniment, but accent the first note of each triplet, as the bass note proper, a trifle more than the other two.

a)

b) Here, of course, only the first eighth-note in each measure should be accented.

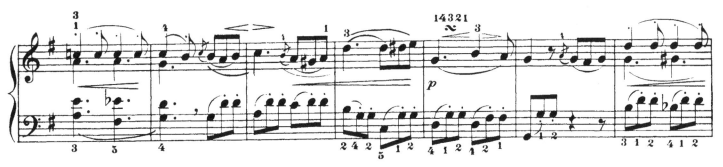

a) From here up to the *ff* discreetly subordinate the left hand throughout (also in the repetitions of the fundamental tone.)

b) Let the *ff* enter abruptly with the fourth eighth-note, without any previous *crescendo*.

SONATA

in G Major

Edited and fingered by
Sigmund Lebert and Hans von Bülow

Ludwig van Beethoven
Op. 49, No. 2

Abbreviations: M.T. signifies Main Theme; S.T., Sub-Theme; Cl.T., Closing Theme; D.G., Development-Group;
R., Return; Tr., Transition; Md.T. Mid-Theme; Ep., Episode.

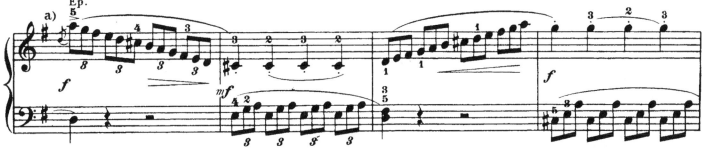

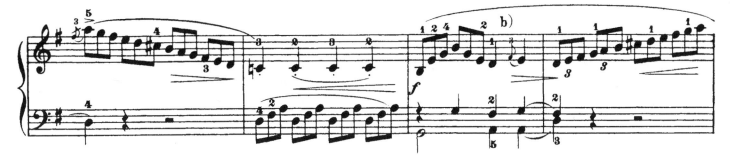

a) Strike all short appoggiaturas on the beat, simultaneously with the accompaniment-note.

b) F# should be executed as a long, accented appoggiatura:

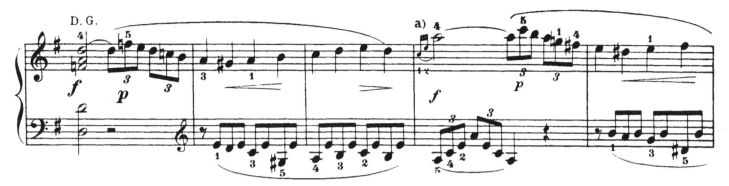

a)

a) ▦ easier: ▦

Tempo di Menuetto. (♩ = 112.)

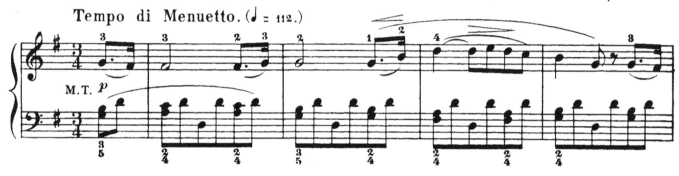

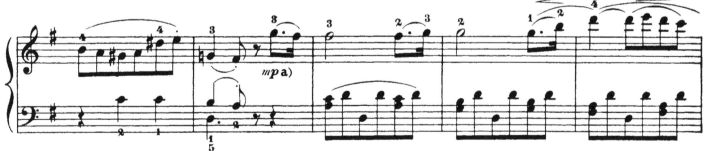

a) *mp* (*mezzo piano*, moderately soft) signifies a degree of tone-power midway between *p* and *mf*.

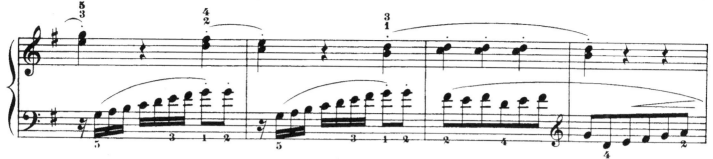

SONATINA
in G Major

Ludwig van Beethoven
Anh. 5, No. 1

Moderato

ROMANZE

SONATINA
in F Major

Ludwig van Beethoven
Anh. 5, No. 2

Allegro assai

RONDO
Allegro

SIX VARIATIONS
on the Duet
"Nel cor più non mi sento" from Giovanni Paisiello's *La Molinara*

Ludwig van Beethoven
WoO 70

(a) Always strike the appoggiatura-note simultaneously with the first accompaniment-note, somewhat shortly, yet without impairing clearness. The accent falls, however, not on the appoggiatura, but on the principal note.

(b) The alterations given by us in small notes, aim at making these variations easily playable by small hands, which cannot yet stretch an octave.

(c) Continue from this movement to the following without interruption of the measure, except when the contrary is indicated by a fermata over the closing double-bar.

Var. I

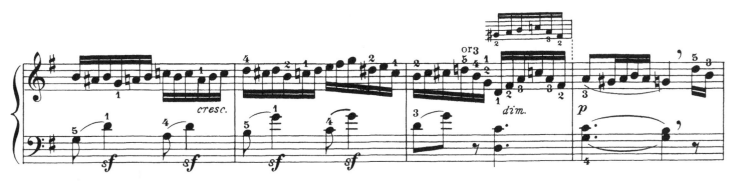

(a) Such a comma indicates a breaking-off somewhat sooner, and a subsequent fresh attack.

(b)

Var. II

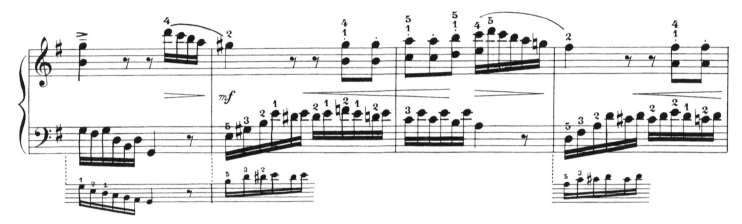

Var. III

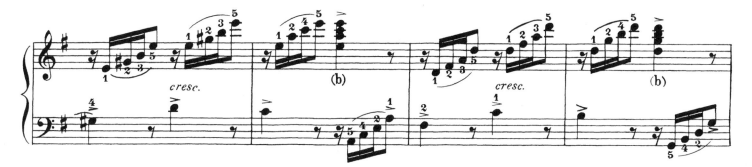

(a) Emphasize the left hand somewhat here, as it has the principal notes of the melody.

(b) Small hands must leave out the lowest tone.

Poco più tranquillo (♪=144)

Var. IV

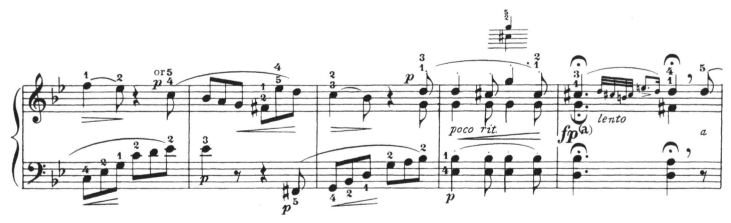

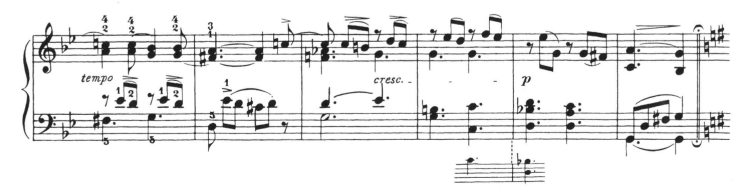

(a) Both the *d-b* in the left hand, as also the *g* in the right, are to be held during the execution of the small notes.

Un pochettino più animato ($\bullet$. = 60)

Var. VI

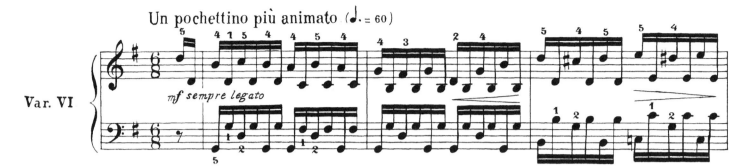

mf sempre legato

p <   *mf*   *cresc.*

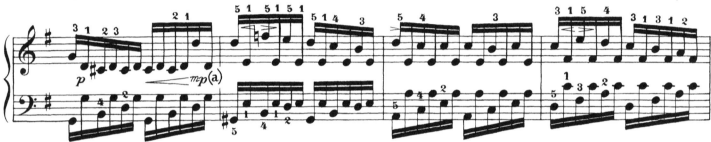

p <   *mp*(a)

cresc.   *poco rit.*   *sf*   *a tempo* p

cresc.

Coda   *m.g.*   *mp*

p *m. d.*

m.g.   *mp*   *poco marcato*

(a)   *mp* (*mezzo piano,* rather softly) signifies a degree of tone-power between p and *mf*

SIX VARIATIONS ON AN ORIGINAL THEME

Edited by Sigmund Lebert

Ludwig van Beethoven
WoO 77

(a) 𝄽 and so, in general, strike all appoggiaturas simultaneously with the accompaniment.

(b) The alterations added by us aim at making these
variations easily playable by small hands which
cannot yet stretch an octave.

(c) By such a comma we indicate that a rhythmical
section must be indicated, and that afterwards a fresh
attack must be made.

(d) *mp* (*mezzo-piano*, rather softly) signifies a degree of tone-power between *p* and *mf*.

(e) Continue from one movement to another without
interruption of the measure, except after Variations
3 and 4.

Var. II.

Var. III.

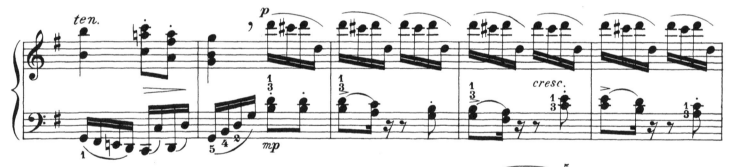

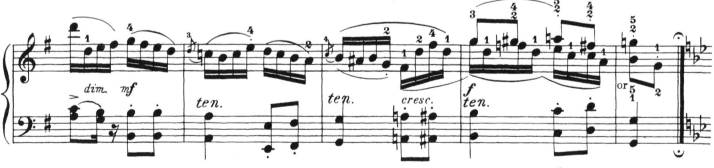

Minore

Poco sostenuto ($\quarternote = 50$)

Var. IV.

Maggiore

Tempo I un poco animato (♩ = 60)

Var. V.

(a) Emphasize the "melody-bearing" highest part.

(b) Strike *b* simultaneously with *c*

Var.VI.

Coda
Tempo I

SIX VARIATIONS ON A SWISS SONG

Ludwig van Beethoven
WoO 64

*) We call special attention to these thoroughly delightful Variations because they are far too little known and appreciated. They will be particularly welcome to *young* pianists.

(a) By a comma we mark those points at which the player ought, by lifting his hands a little earlier than the note-value indicates, to bring out a rhythmical division.

(b) Proceed without interrupting the rhythm; and similarly after Variations 1 and 3.

Minore

Poco sostenuto e doloroso (♩ = 112)

Var. III

Maggiore

Tempo I un poco animato (♩ = 126)

Var. IV

Ped. simile

Var. V

Var. VI

Coda

(a) ♪♪♪♪♪♪ or easier ♪♪♪♪